# Elements of Change
*A Collection of Poetry*

MARY CZERWINSKI

Copyright © 2015 Mary Czerwinski

All rights reserved. No part of this publication may be reproduced, distributed, or transmitted in any form or by any means, including photocopying, recording, or other electronic or mechanical methods, without the prior written permission of the publisher, except in the case of brief quotations embodied in critical reviews and certain other noncommercial uses permitted by copyright law.

Cover Photo Copyright © 2015 Mary Czerwinski
Author Photo Copyright © 2014 Christopher Forbes
Edited by Eva Xanthopoulos, founder of Poehemian Press

Author Contact Information: mongocitymedia@gmail.com

ISBN: 1508880069
ISBN-13: 978-1508880066

**For Leonard Nimoy**
*Actor, Artist, Singer, Poet*

# INTRODUCTION

I truly believe a piece of art should speak for itself. I feel pretentious even calling these fragmented words, art. I hesitated in even writing this introduction. Talking about my work makes me uneasy because you can't take away influence once it's given out. What you get from these words is your own truth. What resonates with you is the feeling you take away. It's unique to you. I may have sewn the words together in descriptive sequences, but your perception is what makes them come to life. That's the great thing about poetry—it deals in the abstract. Your opinion on what the writer is conveying is correct even if it differs from one person to the next. I love poetry for that reason. You mold it to fit your experience. I've often done that with song lyrics or quotations.

I do think it's worth noting that this is a collection of work that has spanned over fifteen years of my life. One experiences a great deal of change during that time. Uncovering old work made me realize how much I have evolved as a writer. In some cases, I would take a single line from an old poem and make it the launching point for an entirely new piece. The one constant in my writing is the use of classical elements. Now, I'm not very new age. I don't pretend to know anything about chakras, but Earth, Air, Fire and Water are within us all and all around us. It seemed to be a natural fit for framing the poems you are about to read.

Over the years, I have had many muses—some real, some imaginary. I fall in love every day. Not in the traditional sense, as that is reserved for a special someone. What I mean is, there are aspects to people and places you encounter that serve as a special kind of inspiration, which opens the floodgates of creativity. I had writer's block for a long time because I thought if everything was going right in my life what could I possibly have to say? As I get older, I realize the opposite is true. The fog of depression suffocates creativity. When you truly get out there amongst nature with friends and observe the world around you, I guarantee there is plenty to write about. This book signifies that fog being lifted, revealing a new era of creativity. *Elements of Change* is deeply personal and is a love letter to living in the moment. Elements are a constant. We are the ones changing and as Heraclitus once said, "Nothing endures but change." I humbly thank you for allowing my words to enter your world. They are yours now.

# TABLE OF CONTENTS

| | |
|---|---|
| *Introduction* | i |
| **Earth** | 1 |
|     Blades of Grass | 3 |
|     Vascular | 4 |
|     Musso & Frank | 5 |
|     Embedded | 6 |
|     The Ballerina | 7 |
|     La Femme | 8 |
| **Air** | 9 |
|     Untitled | 11 |
|     Lost | 12 |
|     Sparkwood & 21 | 13 |
|     Untitled | 14 |
| **Fire** | 15 |
|     The Space Between | 17 |
|     Exposed | 19 |
|     Reunion | 20 |
|     All these things and more... | 21 |
|     Web of Lives | 22 |
| **Water** | 23 |
|     Phototaxis | 25 |
|     Metamorphosis | 26 |
|     Safe Harbor | 27 |
|     Caution Kills More Dreams Than Lack of Talent | 28 |
|     Los Angeles After the Rain | 29 |
|     The Fist | 30 |
|     32 Degrees | 31 |
|     Screaming Silence | 32 |
|     someone I have never kissed, gladly would | 33 |
| *Special Thanks* | 35 |

# EARTH

"The earth laughs in flowers."
-Ralph Waldo Emerson

**Blades of Grass**

Her hair like straw,
creates a haystack in my mind
of images lost like needles,
sharp pins pricking when I enter.

Bales of baggage weigh down her head
outside grassy knolls of dandelions flourish
softening her skull of silence in spring,
spreading pollen in summer.

I tried to beg for forgiveness on bent knee,
but all she did was stain my jeans.
I wish I could mow down her ragged meadow
and plow through the weeds.

**Vascular**

Leaf by leaf
delicately unfolding,
rolling, reaching, stretching
towards the light like a child
eagerly blowing air into a paper noisemaker
that unfurls before midnight.

What becomes a firework of fronds
starts as a wallflower, a shrinking violet
tightly wound up until the moment
youth explodes into prime.

Like a caterpillar uncurling itself
to reveal its speckled underbelly.
Radioactive-green spores
adorn the mighty fern from stipe
to stem like a neon sequined-dress
at a modest affair.

Common houseplant,
salad for dinosaurs,
filler for florists,
invasive weed,
necessary-evil,
remover of arsenic,
ancient fossil fuel
that proves its worth.

Ferns will outlive us all
and have quite the kingdom
with cockroaches once
we're extinct.

One day, we'll be in textbooks
as the species that assumed ferns
needed our care.

We were dead wrong.

**Musso & Frank**

Gin is delightful—
tastes like drinking trees.
*Gin & tonic?*
Effervescent juniper in a glass,
add lime and you're drinking
Christmas in California.

**Embedded**

Promises lost like a ring,
wedged between two cushions,

presumed forgotten, salvaged
but already
replaced.

You said you should live in salt,
but you poured it onto my open
wound.

Once the pain subsided I saw
what you were trying to preserve.

You can destroy the evidence, but not
its DNA.

**The Ballerina**

Words bind like corset's rope—
Each phrase, a gift and a curse
with too many loose ends to tie off

Like some sick music box playing the same tune,
we latch onto the comfort of
a familiar melody, but always
long to hear something new.

Me, the ballerina spinning in circles.
You, the curious kid who keeps opening
the box. When the child moved on,
all the moments replayed in my head.

I tried to shake you off like a dog
shakes rain from its coat,
but your memory stayed damp
like a towel that has yet to dry.

The distorted tune plays on
and hope keeps dancing in these
soft-soled shoes.

## La Femme

At an all-vegan buffet, she is prime rib:
meaty, raw and dripping with sexuality.
A chameleon carnivore stalking its prey
meticulously waiting in the cool, calm absence of reason.

Tragic eyes reveal a child's longing
But in this grim cave they light the way
to redemption in a way religion never could.
I am struck by the sharpness of your defeat.
You drive a pickup truck kissed with rust
while others, less secure, put their faith in foreign modes.

She is all-American grassroots rugged,
Androgynous siren, ruler of the beasts,
A ruby tossed in a never-ending sea of diamonds.

Where there were flowers, she was the weed,
Where that was restraint, she was free.

Her scars mark the highway the tame fear to tread,
Her lips overly ripe, remain unpicked
under the flashing neon of a lonely desert road,
She is the blizzard in the same manner to which she is
volcanic.

Leather clings to the slopes of her womanhood,
as the lava she exudes
consumes the unpaved road to which I call
home.

## AIR
"Music, the mosaic of the air."
- Andrew Marvell

**Untitled**

Of all the things we've exchanged,
it's the simplicity of shared breath
that I cherish the most.

Between the ellipsis of
conversations,
the annoyance of snores
and the promises of
kisses layered,
we are one in the
sharing of air.

I am as important to you,
as you are to me.
We fill each other's
lungs with an essential need.

And in this moment, I take
in your oxygen and sigh.

## Lost

Lost in a tinsel forest,
I comb through splintered ends
seeking a lifeline evicted in this lifetime.
Does your déjà vu deceive you?

If you were waiting for me,
your patience ran thin like stockings
wavering in a December breeze.

But hope is a dangerous drug,
and memory is a demon I can't exorcise,
Doubt steals from possibility
and I'm stuck fighting ghosts of regret.

Faith is fleeting,
but patience is a bridge
joining the wait with "what if?"
But then I remember,
recollection is unreliable like
asking for directions.
And so I take the chance
and cross the stream
sprung from a fountain of futility.

I skip rocks off river's edge
and watch the fantails of fish
as night draws near. And if I
can't sleep in the wilderness,
I will find that special star to wish on.
I will connect the dots of your stubble
and when I wake, may it scratch me,
so I know I'm not dreaming.

**Sparkwood & 21**

Shadows dissect the night,
Diamonds cut the sky,
Off-kilter treading
on uneven terrain,
Perfection in assemblage,
Momentary lapse of judgment
slices barriers built by years.
In a singular decision,
existence will never be the same.

Nature's electricity illuminates the view,
Chemicals commingle consciences,
Hope flickers through trees,
Souls separated for centuries
balance with perfect symmetry,
Fear no longer dictates where
secrets are stored.
Devouring the moment—
we are addicts to the unknown.

**Untitled**

I scoured your letters and retraced our steps,
studied the depth of your eyes & roadmaps
of lines.

I played our songs on repeat listening
for a hidden message in the melody.

I see you on the street in the faces
of strangers and the in the light
of the stars.

I'm in love with a ghost, your timeless specter.
Your haunting visage,
your everlasting scars

I focused my thoughts to the wind,
but reason is a kite tethered to the ground.
I reached your heights, but
always came back down.

# FIRE

"Poetry is just the evidence of life.
If your life is burning well, poetry is just the ash."
-Leonard Cohen

## The Space Between

Glances burning,
Images stirring,
Charred black remains
left in our wake,
Some struggle with matches
to find a single spark,
Others are born of fire & may
never go dark.

Across a room and still connected
are the unspoken words in our eyes.
Your smile closes the gap between our
lives.

Can we meet in the space between?
Let's fill the void and make time stand still,
Let's blow off life and surrender to how we feel,
I'm always lingering
in the wild rush of words so easily erased.

You are the lines I always had in my head,
but couldn't deliver.
You cure me of this codependent stutter.
When the story seemed in circles,
you broke through and set me straight.
In the clack of the keyboard and the fluidity of ink,
you are rushing onto a page.

In my blurred scribbles, I search for the marks I asked
you not to leave, a desperate attempt to find
fingerprints that never appear.

Stolen seconds across divisions of time
extinguishing breath from crowded rooms,
Consuming my mind with boundless thoughts.

Can we meet in the void?
Do you think the world will see our glow?
Would it be too revealing if we let them know?
My heart reels from a thousand affirmations so
easily dismissed.

Sometimes I wish I could stare into the eternity
of our eyes and capture the essence of desire.
I want to fill notebooks with thick black ink outlining
how we conspire.

In the end,
it's the imprints you've left on memory that
cannot be replaced.

**Exposed**

I am naked
in your presence.
Your stare surrounds my intangible innocence.
Suddenly each vein seems to pulse its purple flow,
pushing forth an awkward shudder,
as I struggle to look into your lens.

You don't notice my hesitation
because I shroud it in a heightened
state of banter, which draws forth
disingenuous laughter.

I attempt to take control by surprising you
with a lascivious gesture or perhaps a joke or two.
You return the favor with deep determination to
get to the bottom of me.

I am paralyzed by your confidence as you tell
tales of one-night-stands in Europe.
I pretend I am cool enough to handle it,
but deep down I lose it.

The table becomes interesting, the clock captivating
"My… How this is the best drink I've ever had."

Then no one speaks and in that moment we are equal,
in clumsy portals of complexity, but it never lasts.

Someone always takes focus.
Someone always frames it just right.

**Reunion**

Sometimes I feel so close to you like we've been here before. Maybe Plato was right and we were once one and circumstance severed us like Siamese twins sharing the same beating heart. My soul searched for a wholeness I never knew could be filled. I felt like a magician's assistant who actually got sawed in half. There was always something amiss. Could there be a mirror somewhere in the attic of my mind that reflected my twin flame like a vampire who finally sees himself? And when I met you for the first time, your gaze confirmed that we were simply reunited and our hearts were mimicking the rhythm from another life.

**All these things and more...**

I am the secrets you take to the grave

I am the dirt swept under the rug

I am the skeletons that dress your closet

I am the faded silhouette of sentiment

I am the last leg of summer that feels like a dream

I am the restless night painted with vivid scenes

I am the focus that's lost while you're at work

I am the hint of a chemical fingerprint left upon your chin

I am the flashing of your heart smeared across your cheek

I am the transfer of excitement felt from afar

I am your divine complement mirrored back at you

I am the emotional mimicry you don't realize you're doing

I am the speech you rehearsed and still forgot

I am Friday night dressed in Sunday's best

I am a record on repeat that you swore you threw out

I am the action figure that was worth more in the box

I am the fantasy
that should have been left
as such.

**Web of Lives**

Let the honey drip,
make the walls blush.

Let them all talk,
make them all watch.

Consume my essence,
destroy all the boundaries.

Head towards me,
never look back.

Dive into the darkness,
drive your point home.

# WATER

"All good writing is swimming under water and holding your breath."
- F. Scott Fitzgerald

**Phototaxis**

Brake lights on shiny black asphalt—
The motion picture kind,
Slick and reflective
like the back of a lizard
emerging from a Louisiana
swamp.

India ink-soaked pavement
absorbing colors and bouncing
them back into a pool of crimson.

Signals shift,
creating a shallow pond
of glossy emerald paint
strewn between intersections framed
by orbs of faded streetlights.
They flicker off and on,
just like the ones mom pointed to
when she said, "be home before dark."

Softly buzzing deathtraps for
insects seeking moonlight.
Directionless they spiral,
so dazzled by artifice
they don't realize
the very thing that
attracts them will
imprison them.

Yet, we, so much more
evolved,
fail to learn from this lesson
&
fall prey to all
myriad of colors
that dance in the night
and evaporate by dawn.

## Metamorphosis

An edgy piece of coral
washed upon the shore
from somewhere deep and dark
on the ocean floor.

Rough to touch and full of
holes.

Sharply unique, but murky in color
from being buried beneath
the sand.

It remained on the beach—
Sun up and sun down until
it became the starkest shade of white.
The perpetual lapping of waves
smoothed its surface
making it safe to touch and bring home.

It is in its loss of color that it becomes
prized like a lobster only known for its
boiled state. Does one ever value the
caterpillar more than the butterfly?

**Safe Harbor**

I can't break free from the dread
of drowning in a safe harbor
with pretty painted boats with perfect names.

The water is so shallow here.
They will all laugh at me.

The yacht club is hardly
open water and crashing waves,
but equally harsh on a novice sailor.

I thought if I were to drown
it would be in the depths
of a sunken pirate ship
in search of some myth spun in gold.

I was waiting to fight
through kelp and dingy water
because the treasure beckons me.

However unobtainable this legend seems,
I would be the one to unearth it,
to dig that much deeper than the next girl
and try just a little harder
than all the rest whose skeletons float beside me.

There is freedom in the pursuit of possibility,
but instead, I play it safe and you play
it safe too.

Fear tethers me to the dock,
while yours anchors you to the bottom
like a concrete block.
We fight against it, but it's useless—
two ships that won't even pass in the night.

## Caution Kills More Dreams Than Lack of Talent

You are not the sum of someone else's expectations,
You are stardust and subversion kicked in the gut,
by the way things ought to be.

You are the child that threatened to run away,
but spent a single shivering night in their treehouse
staring at their bedroom window cooking up apologies.

I know the allure of looking out, but never seeing the horizon.
I've been the kid who gets to the edge of the diving board
and can't jump in.
Knees lock, fear shakes and grabs hold of you.
The more you fight it, the more you slip.

If you just trusted your initial impulse, you'd be
laughing at the bottom urging others to the warm water
that envelopes and buoys your uncertainty.

Float freely instead of always sinking your soul with what might
go wrong.

**Los Angeles After the Rain**

Like LA after the rain
unbelievable clarity
electric green hillsides
soft blue skies
visibility for miles
oceanic horizons
fertile ground at our feet
Tread lightly—
these sparse forms
of life have not matured
enough to handle trampling.

Be thankful for this mudslide
as dry spells are always around the corner.

**The Fist**

I am a fist,
which clenches shut and releases wide,
A soft clamshell
gently opening and closing
to absorb emotional nourishment
in the great deep of indifference.

I am a fist,
veins popping, ready for action,
Sullied knuckles of dried blood—
A veneer of healing flesh
still stinging when you rinse it,
A scab that has yet to form.

I am a fist,
holding your hand tight when you are lost,
guiding you through crowded rooms
and across lanes of asphalt riddled with potholes.

Reassurance links your palm to mine,
A diversion of cool confidence distracts you from my sweat.

## 32 Degrees

I'm running hard on this treadmill
afraid of the cold, cruel ground.
I push forward, not realizing
I've been still.

Alone on the trail,
I see the distant future,
but the path leads to nowhere.
I blindly head in a new direction,
leaving doubt in the dust.
Wind rips salt from my focused eyes.
Everything darkens all at once,
The match routinely blows out,
There is no shelter from the wind.

I look down at the snow-packed
sidewalk. Each step crunches, knees buckle
as soles hit the frozen concrete.
Fear engages a staggering heartbeat,
Water slowly breaks down cement
as words do to my walls.

A figure appears out of nowhere like mist,
I slow my pace to a cautious gait
and let the moisture seep in. I imagine myself
frozen in this moment.

The constant freezing up and spreading out
aid your persistent molecules in locking with
mine. Let's share electrons and push out
together. So what if this beautiful hexagon
eventually forms a pothole?
We're in this together now.

At least,
until Spring…

**Screaming Silence**

You move through me like water,
You cleanse heartache from my soul.
How foolish words can be when we act
selfishly.

Your silence is powerful like strong, shiny
steel.
Your quiet face is the loudest sound I have
ever heard.

Glassy martini eyes burn my heart with
every
drop.

**someone I have never kissed, gladly would**
**(in the style of e.e. cummings)**

someone I have never kissed, gladly would
if given the chance, your lips pout sadness:
in your most innocent smile are promises which devour me,
or which I cannot keep because fantasy excites more than reality

your glittering eyelash envelopes me
though I have built a wall from contact,
you scale it always brick by brick as a spider crawls
up a window to glance inside
(climbing sneakily, calmly) seeking warmth

or if your desire is to catapult over me, I and
my fear will provide a safety net to catch the fall
as when a widow spins a web waiting gently for
its victim to become entangled

nothing can explain to others this pull
you have in your most meaningless grin: whose meaning
drives me to construct this divide, which places
us opposite with each other

(i do not know what is about you that builds
and breaks off; only something in me knows
the message of your lips is clearer than pure water)
nobody, not even spiders, can cut through water without getting soaked.

# SPECIAL THANKS

Melanie P. Falina, John Champion, Ashley Labrie, Steve Newman, Connor Bright, Stacy Sholes, Christopher Forbes, Brandt Kofton and my parents.